MA

The Timetraveller's Guide to . . .

SHAKESPEARE'S
LONDON

First published in 2004 by Watling St Publishing

The Glen

Southrop

Lechlade

Gloucestershire

GL7 3NY

Printed in Italy

ISBN 1-904153-10-0

24681097531

Mackerel Limited

Illustrations: Mark Davis

www.tempus-publishing.com

MA	MB	MC
MD	ME	MF
MG	MH	MM
MN	MO	MR
AB	MT	MW

The Timetraveller's Guide to . . .

SHAKESPEARE'S LONDON

Joshua Doder

WATLING STREET

Joshua Doder lives in London with his wife, two dogs, three cats and a ferret called Miki. He has worked as a chef, a librarian and an actor. His hobbies include collecting Japanese pottery and climbing mountains. He is now writing a short history of pizza.

Contents

INTRODUCTION

The year is 1596. Your name is Tom Barnsley. You are twelve years old. You work for a merchant in the City of London. He sits upstairs, counting his coins, while you carry bales of cloth around the basement.

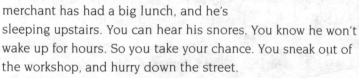

Today is a warm Tuesday afternoon in June. Now, it's one o'clock in the afternoon. The merchant has had a big lunch, and he's sleeping upstairs. You can hear his snores. You know he won't wake up for hours. So you take your chance. You sneak out of the workshop, and hurry down the street.

You walk through the city, hurry over the bridge, and go into Southwark. At the end of a dingy street, you find a queue of people, waiting outside a doorway. You join the queue. You wait. The queue shuffles forward. When you reach the front, you pay a penny and go through the door.

Now, you're inside a large, round building which has no roof. Two or three hundred people are milling around. The rich ones sit on benches around the sides. The poor ones – like you – stand up in the middle, pressing against the stage.

You stand there for ten minutes. People push and shove. A woman has a basket of fruit. She shouts: 'Who wants to buy my oranges? Luverly oranges! Who'll buy my luverly oranges? Only a penny for five!'

Then a man walks onto the stage.

He's wearing clothes made from gold, and carrying a long sword.

He starts talking.

Another man walks onto the stage. They talk together.

The play has started.

You watch. The play is brilliant. It's funny, and clever, and exciting.

About an hour into the play, you notice someone standing at the side of the stage. A man. He's thirty-five or forty. He never moves or speaks. He just watches the action.

You watch him for a minute. He has a big, bald forehead like a shiny egg. On his chin, there's a little goatee beard. His bright eyes focus intently on the stage, watching the play. He never laughs at the funny lines. He never looks sad or tense. He just watches and listens.

From the way that he is watching, you might guess that he was involved with the play. You might think that he was the producer, or the director, or even the writer.

You don't know it, but you're right.

That man is the writer of the play. Five hundred years from now, no one will remember the name of Tom Barnsley. No one will even know that Tom Barnsley ever existed. But everyone will know about this man, this writer. Everyone will know his name.

CHAPTER ONE

Stratford to London

In 1564, William Shakespeare was born in Stratford-upon-Avon, a small town roughly in the middle of England. No one knows the exact date of his birthday, but people sometimes celebrate it on 23 April. We know from the parish records that he was baptised on 26 April, and he was probably born two or three days before he was baptised. So, perhaps his birthday really was 23 April.

The Shakespeare family lived in Henly Street, which was right in the middle of Stratford. William's father, John Shakespeare, was a glover. In other words, he made gloves. He must have been very good at making gloves, because he earned a lot of money, and eventually became the Mayor of Stratford.

William's mother was called Mary Arden. Together, John and Mary Shakespeare had eight children. Three of them died young. Four lived, but have been forgotten. And one of them is still remembered today, four hundred and fifty years later. Every day, somewhere around the world, his words will be spoken. His plays are performed in every country on the planet. Everyone knows his name.

Married with Children

When William Shakespeare was eighteen, he married a local woman called Anne Hathaway. They had three children: two girls, Susanna and Judith, and a boy, Hamnet. Shakespeare wasn't much more than twenty years old, but he already had a family to support. He had five mouths to feed: himself, his wife, and three children. What should he do? What could he do? He ran away.

No one knows why Shakespeare fled from Stratford and travelled to London. There is a legend that he had to run away because he was caught poaching deer from a nobleman's estate. There is another legend that a travelling band of actors stopped in Stratford, where they performed a play; Shakespeare was so thrilled by the actors that, when they packed their bags, he travelled down to London with them and became an actor too. However, no one knows if either of these legends is true. Perhaps Shakespeare simply didn't want to spend the rest of his life in Stratford-upon-Avon. Perhaps he decided that he didn't like his wife. Or perhaps he just wanted to see London – the biggest and most exciting city in England. For whatever reason, he left his home and his family, and headed south.

Along the M40

From Stratford-upon-Avon to London is a distance of one hundred and two miles. Nowadays, you could do this journey by car or train. It would take about two hours. If you went by car, you'd whizz almost all the way along a motorway called the M40.

For Shakespeare, things were more difficult. Most likely, he walked. If he walked quite quickly, he would have done the journey in four days.

Four days? Today, a Japanese tourist could get from Tokyo to Stratford in less than four days. An American tourist could leave New York in the morning, get to London in the afternoon, and reach Stratford by the evening. The world has got much faster. Every day, Shakespeare walked through beautiful fields and thick forests. He saw hundreds of birds and animals. The air in his lungs was clean and fresh.

Every night, Shakespeare stayed in an inn, where he would have hired a bed for a penny. Nowadays, a room in a bed & breakfast on his route, in Woodstock or High Wycombe say, would probably cost forty pounds. That's four thousand pennies! For that price, Shakespeare could have stayed four thousand nights in an inn. Four thousand nights is ten years, eleven months and twenty days. He'd never have got to London!

Talk of the Town

'London is the capital of England and so superior to other English towns that London is not said to be in England, but rather England to be in London, for England's most resplendent objects may be seen in and around London: so that he who sightsees London and the royal courts in its vicinity may assert without impertinence that he is properly acquainted with England.'

That was written by a man called Thomas Platter, who travelled from Switzerland to London in the 1590s. Thomas Platter went to the theatre several times, and left some descriptions of plays that he had seen, some of which were written by Shakespeare.

In Shakespeare's time, London was much smaller than it is today. For instance, Islington and Charing Cross were little villages. If you wanted a nice day out, you might go to

Hampstead, Highgate or Crouch Hill, where you could walk through the forests, and get some fresh air.

As Shakespeare got closer to the city, he would have noticed all the houses. Most of them were small and low. Spiked among them, there were a hundred and twenty church spires, like needles pointing at the sky. In the centre, there was the tall, graceful shape of the old St Paul's Cathedral, then the most impressive building in the whole of England.

Before Shakespeare reached the city, he would have passed the gallows at Tyburn. Gallows are a wooden structure used to hang people. Every week, criminals would be sentenced to death and hanged from the gallows. The place where the gallows stood is now called Marble Arch, and it is a busy roundabout.

From Tyburn, Shakespeare would have walked through the city walls and into London. The walls had seven gates. If you look on a map of London, you will still see the names of these gates, although the actual gates have disappeared. They are Aldgate, Bishopsgate, Moorgate, Cripplegate, Aldersgate, Newgate and Ludgate. The entire length of the walls was about two miles, which you could probably walk in about 45 minutes. Today, it would take more than 45 hours to walk round London.

In Shakespeare's time the walls were not used as protection, because no one had tried to attack London for many years. In fact, they didn't really have any practical purpose. However, the gates were closed at night.

So, Shakespeare would have walked through one of the gates, and into the city of London. What did he find next?

Stow the Surveyor

On 8 April 1605, an old man named John Stow died at the grand old age of eighty. Not long after his death, his widow paid for a monument, which was erected in the Church of St Andrew Undershaft in the City of London. You can still visit this church and see the statue of John Stow's head.

Why would you want to? Why would anyone wish to remember John Stow? Well, living for eighty years was a great achievement in the sixteenth century, but John Stow achieved something else too: he made a survey of London which, since that time, has helped historians when they try to imagine what life must have been like in Shakespeare's London.

John Stow's Survey of London was first published in 1598. On its pages, you will discover a huge amount of information about London in the 1590s. If you travelled back in time, and wanted a guidebook to the city, John Stow's Survey is the book that you would use. In the Church of St Andrew Undershaft, the statue of John Stow shows an old man

holding a quill in his hands. He is writing. The statue is made from stone, but the quill is a clean, white feather. It doesn't look five hundred years old, and it isn't. Every year, on 5 April, the Lord Mayor of London comes to the Church of St Andrew Undershaft with all his Sheriffs, and places a new quill in the statue's hands. If the statue suddenly came to life, John Stow would find himself well equipped to start writing immediately.

CHAPTER TWO

Arriving in the City

When Shakespeare entered the gates, he noticed one thing before anything else: the SMELL. Having come from the countryside, he was almost knocked down by the sheer stink of London's streets.

People dumped their rubbish in the street. And not just rubbish. People peed in the street. They even pooed in the street. Dogs peed and pooed in the streets. Horses peed and pooed in the streets. Donkeys, mules, cows and chickens peed and pooed in the streets. Now you can see why London smelled so terrible!

The first time that Shakespeare walked through the streets of London, what else did he notice? (Apart from the ATROCIOUS STINK.)

Firstly, he noticed all the pubs. Almost every street had a pub. Londoners obviously liked beer. In fact, it wasn't safe to drink the water in London. Tea and coffee had recently been introduced but they were very, very expensive and ordinary people couldn't afford to buy them. So rather than drinking water, tea or coffee, people drank beer.

To make beer, you have to boil water, which gets rid of germs. That's why it was safe to drink. So, everyone drank beer, and no one touched water. Even children drank two or three pints of beer every day – but the beer was much weaker than it is today, so they didn't get drunk. Only very small children would drink milk instead of beer.

Secondly, Shakespeare noticed that the streets were very narrow. They weren't like the modern streets of London, which have room for two cars going in different directions and pedestrians on either side of the road. In 1590, the streets were just wide enough for a horse and a cart.

Thirdly, he noticed all the people. Hundreds of them! Thousands of them! Shakespeare had never seen so many people in one place. London was the biggest city in Britain, and it had a population of somewhere between 100,000 and 200,000 people. Every year, more people came to live in the city. By the time that Shakespeare finally left London, the population had grown to half a million. Since then, it has kept growing. (Do you know how many people live in London today? I'll give you a clue. It's a lot more than two hundred thousand. In fact, it's several million more. About 7 million people live in London today.)

Of these two hundred thousand Londoners, most were English, but there were also many Scots, Welsh and Irish too, plus a few French, Dutch, Spaniards and Italians. So, Shakespeare was surrounded by lots of different accents and lots of different languages.

As he walked around London, he discovered that the city was divided by four main streets:

Firstly, the road from Newgate to Aldgate.

Secondly, the road from Bishopsgate to the south side of the river, crossing over London Bridge.

Thirdly, the road from Ludgate to the Tower of London, going around St Paul's Cathedral.

Fourthly, Thames Street, which ran alongside the river from Blackfriars to the Tower of London.

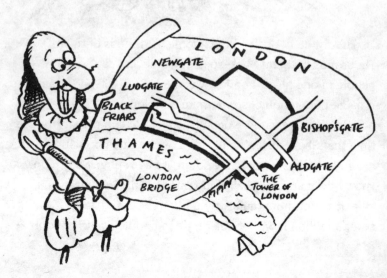

No one knows what Shakespeare did when he first arrived in London. How did he earn a living? Where did he find to sleep? What did he eat? However, there is a legend that describes his first job in the city. According to this myth, he worked outside one of the theatres, looking after the horses that belonged to noblemen who had come to see the plays.

Bringing Water to the City.

If you lived in London, it was very difficult to get clean water. The houses didn't have taps or water pipes. Instead, men walked the streets, selling water from buckets and barrels that they carried on their backs. They were called water carriers.

In 1580, the city authorities decided that they should do something about the lack of water. So they built a river to bring water from the countryside to London. They called it THE NEW RIVER. It flowed from Enfield to the centre of London. If you go to North London, you can still see the New River. It flows through Wood Green, Finsbury Park, Stoke Newington and Islington. Nowadays, you wouldn't want to drink from it. You wouldn't even want to have a bath in it. The riverwater is brown and full of weeds.

THE FANCY LADY'S GUIDE TO SHOPS IN LONDON

BY OUR SHOPPING CORRESPONDENT JEMIMA PINK~GUSSETT

Shopping in our great city is very easy. Just look for the name of the street, and you will discover what you can buy there.

If you go to Bread Street, you will find the bakers. For milk, you should go to Milk Street. For gold, walk down to Goldsmith's Row. If you want to buy some fish, you should go to Friday Street. (For foreigners who don't understand our habits, I should explain that we eat fish on Fridays.)

Throughout the city, every different profession has its own area. Drapers lay out their cloth in Watling Street. Candlemakers will be found in Candlewick Street. Skinners sharpen their knives in Walbrook. Shoemakers stitch their leather in Cordwainer Street. Butchers wield their cleavers in Eastcheep. Booksellers piled their volumes in the churchyard of St Paul's Cathedral.

CHAPTER THREE

The First Theatres

During the first half of the sixteenth century, actors didn't perform plays in theatres, for one very simple reason. There weren't any theatres. No one had built them yet. So, they performed in pubs. If you wanted to watch a play, you went to the pub and bought a drink. The drinkers would sit on benches or stand up, holding their pints of beer, and the actors would perform.

In Shoreditch there was a pub called the Bull Tavern. A group of actors performed in the courtyard. Their boss was a man named James Burbage. He and his two sons were the greatest theatrical impresarios in British history.

An IMPRESARIO is a showman who arranges entertainments for an audience. He is the producer of a theatre company or an opera company. So, James Burbage assembled a group of actors. Every day, they performed a play in the courtyard of The Bull Tavern. They performed in Shoreditch because it was outside the walls of the city. By law, no actors were allowed to perform within the walls of London.

Over the years, James Burbage became more and more successful. Finally, he realized that he would have to stop putting on plays in the pub. Instead, he would have to build a place specially for plays.

It was the first theatre in London. Can you guess what it was called? There were no other theatres in London, so its name was very simple. It was called 'The Theatre'.

The Theatre was made of wood and brick. It cost £700 pounds to build. Every day, people came to see plays there, and paid one penny each. As you can imagine, James Burbage waited a long time get his £700 back again.

The second theatre to be built in Britain was only a couple of minutes' walk away. It was called the Curtain. If the Theatre was sold out, you could go to the Curtain instead.

Shakespeare's Boys

One day, a young man started working at the Theatre. His name was William Shakespeare.

No one knows why or how Shakespeare got involved in the theatre. Perhaps he just turned up and asked for a job. If so, he arrived at the right time. The theatre was booming. Every week, the audiences were bigger.

There is another old tradition which says that Shakespeare didn't work as an actor. Instead, he worked with horses. People rode to the theatre on horseback, and they needed someone to look after their horses while they watched the play. That was Shakespeare's job. The tradition says that Shakespeare became very successful – so successful, in fact, that he could hire a group of boys to work for him. They were called 'Shakespeare's Boys'.

The actors from the Theatre lived nearby. If you have a London A–Z, you can look up the streets where they lived. Shakespeare lived on Shoreditch High Street. James Burbage's son, Richard, lived in Holywell Lane, and so did John Webster, who was also a famous playwright. Christopher Marlowe, another famous writer, lived in Norton Folgate. (You will discover more about Marlowe in Chapter 10.)

A Boy Playing a Girl Playing a Boy

There were no actresses in Elizabethan plays. Only men were allowed to act on the stage. So, the parts of women were played by young boys of twelve or thirteen. In several of his plays, Shakespeare has some fun with this. The men often dress up as women and vice versa. In *As You Like It*, for instance, Rosalind disguises herself as a boy. Therefore, the audience would have watched a boy dressed as a girl playing a girl disguised as a boy!

In 1597, James Burbage died. His sons Cuthbert and Richard quarrelled with their landlord, who owned the land that the Curtain was built on. The landlord threatened to pull down the theatre and use the timber for firewood. So, one night just after Christmas, Richard and Cuthbert Burbage went to the theatre with a group of their friends. They pulled down the building, but they didn't burn the timber. Instead, they carried it through London, crossed the river, and went to Southwark, where they used the same timber to build a new theatre.

50 Million Visits to the Theatre

Between the 1560s, when the first theatres were established in London, and 1642, when all the theatres were forced to close, over 50 million visits were made to theatres. This might mean that one person went 50 million times. Or it could mean that 50 million people each went once. Or it could mean that half a million people each went to the theatre a hundred times. Which do you think is more likely?

Why did they choose Southwark? You'll find out if you keep reading. But first, let's look at the route that they would have taken, that chilly day, as they carried piles of wood from North London to South London.

CHAPTER FOUR

The River

Richard and Cuthbert Burbage put their new theatre on the south side of the river Thames in a place called Southwark. To cross the river, you walked over the bridge or you took a boat.

But you didn't just use boats to cross the river. They were also the quickest way to travel round London. The streets were so narrow, and packed with so many people, that it took a long time to get from one place to another by walking. It was much quicker to jump in a boat. You would pay the boatman, and he would row you along the river to your destination.

The price of your journey depended on two things: how far you were going, and which way the tide was flowing. If you travelled in the same direction as the tide, you would go quickly, so your journey would be cheap. If you travelled against the tide, you would go slowly, and your journey would be more expensive.

Thousands of men earned their living on the river. Imagine all the taxis and buses which travel through modern London, picking up passengers. The river was the same. Crowded with little boats, searching for passengers who wanted to cross from one side to the other, or travel quickly to a different part of the city.

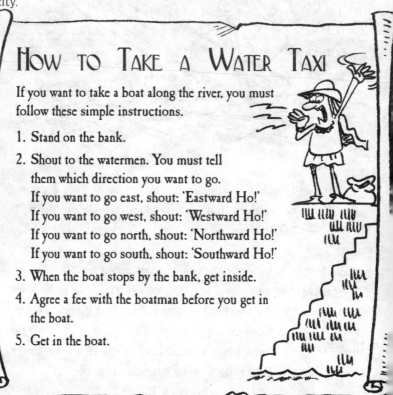

How to Take a Water Taxi

If you want to take a boat along the river, you must follow these simple instructions.

1. Stand on the bank.
2. Shout to the watermen. You must tell them which direction you want to go.
   If you want to go east, shout: 'Eastward Ho!'
   If you want to go west, shout: 'Westward Ho!'
   If you want to go north, shout: 'Northward Ho!'
   If you want to go south, shout: 'Southward Ho!'
3. When the boat stops by the bank, get inside.
4. Agree a fee with the boatman before you get in the boat.
5. Get in the boat.

John Taylor's River Rhymes

At Queenhithe, there was a pub called the Red Knight. This was the meeting-place for the London watermen. They would discuss river business and complain about how little they got paid. Their wages had been set by Queen (Bloody) Mary, and they hadn't been raised since. Just like modern taxi drivers, the watermen probably grumbled about everything: the weather, foreigners, politics, and how things used to be better in the old days.

The most famous of the watermen was called John Taylor.

John Taylor was born in 1580, and went to London when he was a teenager. He joined the navy, and travelled around the world a little. Then he returned to London, and started working as a boatman. Perhaps Shakespeare once took a trip in his boat. Perhaps they talked about poetry. One day, John Taylor decided that he wanted to be more than just a waterman; he wanted to be a poet too.

In his poems, he describes some of the interesting things that he did. For instance, he decided to sail from London to Queenborough in a paper boat. He built a boat from paper. He launched it onto the River Thames. He got inside, and started padding. The boat sank. Although the journey wasn't exactly successful, John Taylor wrote a funny poem about it.

Another of his poems is called *The Penniless Pilgrimage*. To gather material for that poem, he travelled around England and Scotland without any money. If he was hungry, he asked someone to give him some food. If he was tired, he asked someone to lend him a bed. To everyone's surprise, John Taylor travelled around the whole country like this, and came back to London, where he wrote a poem about his adventures. This is the full title of that poem: *The Pennylesse Pilgrimage; or, the Moneylesse Perambulation of John Taylor, alias the Kings Magesties Water-Poet; How He TRAVAILED on Foot from London to Edenborough in Scotland, Not Carrying any Money To or Fro, Neither Begging, Borrowing, or Asking Meate, Drinke, or Lodging.* Catchy eh?

Englishmen Abroad

When Shakespeare wasn't working in the theatre, writing a play or performing, he would have been talking to men like John Taylor. Perhaps he walked down to the port, which was full of people and produce from all around the world. He would have heard amazing stories. He would have talked to men who had travelled to the other side of the world.

In the 1580s and 1590s, Englishmen voyaged all around the world. In India, Libya, Russia and Turkey, the English were trading. In Peru and Chile, the English were stealing from the Spanish. And when they had finished, they sailed back to England, and stopped for a pint of good English beer beside the river Thames.

From their stories, Shakespeare invented his own visions of cities and countries around the world. He wrote about real places like Venice, Padua and Verona. He also invented his own places, such as the island in *The Tempest*.

Shakespeare wasn't very good at geography. He made lots of mistakes in his plays. In *Two Gentlemen of Verona*, people get a boat from Verona – but the city is actually miles from the sea. In *The Taming of the Shrew*, someone lands a boat at Padua – which is even further from the sea. Therefore, Shakespeare probably hadn't actually been to these places. He had just heard about them from other people. He had been talking to sailors or explorers, and later, when he came to write his plays, he misremembered what they had told him.

New Foods from Foreign Land

When Walter Raleigh sailed to America, he returned with two amazing new plants: firstly, a knobbly round thing; secondly, a bush with lots of leaves.

What was the knobbly round thing?
It grew in the ground. You take several of them into the kitchen, and cook them. You could boil them, roast them or fry them. You could mash them. You could even make them into chips – although that might be difficult, because no one had invented a deep-fat fryer yet. Do you know what they were?

What was the bush with lots of leaves?
You pick the leaves, and dry them in the sun. Then you put them in a pipe, and set fire to them. When they burnt slowly, they made a smoke, which some people thought tasted nice. Can you guess the name of the plant?

THE DAILY THUNDER

London's finest newspaper   3 September 1592

EXPLORER RETURNS WITH
'TOMATO'
OPINIONS DIVIDED ON WHAT IT IS.

Yesterday, a ship returned from the Americas after a voyage of seven months. Among the other wonders from that strange land, the sailors brought a small, round, red fruit. They say it is called a tomato. Apparently, tomatoes can be added to a salad. They are said to be tasty. Several of the Queen s priests have been testing this tomato, and, in their opinion, it should be taken straight back to America where it belongs. Other sources suggest making the tomato into soup. (Story continued on page 3.)

Also in this issue:

The River Thames Café Cookbook

*by Cuthbert Oliver,
Chef to Her Royal Highness*

*Lovely recipes using ingredients fresh
from the New World*

Tobacco Omelette

*Make an omelette. Put the
tobacco inside. Eat it quickly
before it gets cold.*

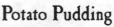

Potato Pudding

*Take three potatoes, and cut them in half.
Put them in a large dish.
Cover them with sugar. Add some
vanilla essence. Bake
for three hours. Eat
with whipped cream.
Pukka.*

The Great Francis Drake

When Shakespeare arrived in London, Francis Drake was a hero. Why? Because he defeated the Spanish Armada in 1588. You can read about the Spanish Armada in lots of other books, so I won't describe it here. However, what matters is this: when Shakespeare came to London, the city was full of men who had fought the Spanish AND WON. The English were triumphant. There was a general feeling that the English could do anything, win anything, beat anyone, and generally rule the world. It was a good time to be English.

A few years before Shakespeare arrived in London, Francis Drake had sailed around the world in his ship, the Golden Hinde. By the 1590s, the Golden Hinde was moored in Deptford, on the south side of the river Thames. Slowly, day by day, year by year, the Golden Hinde's old wood was rotting away.

CHAPTER FIVE

London Bridge and Southwark

If you didn't cross the river by boat, or swim, then you had to go across London Bridge. It was the only bridge in London. There have been many different bridges called London Bridge. The first was built by the Romans, who made it from wood. The most recent is made of concrete, and it opened in 1973. It was probably the first one – the wooden Roman one – which burnt down. As the song says:

> *London Bridge is burning down, burning down.*
> *London Bridge is burning down, my fair lady.*

In Shakespeare's time, London Bridge was made of stone. That was to stop it burning down again. The bridge had twenty arches, and it was originally built in 1176. So, it had already been standing for four hundred years when Shakespeare arrived. All along the bridge, there were buildings. They had two storeys. On the ground floor, there were shops, so people walking across the bridge would be tempted to stop and buy something. People lived on the top floors. In the very middle of the bridge, there was a chapel and a drawbridge, which could be lifted to let big ships pass further up the river.

Do you remember that each part of London was associated with a different profession? It was the pinmakers who had their shops on London Bridge. That's where you went if you wanted to buy some pins.

The bridge had a gate at each end. Every night, these gates were locked at nine o'clock. Therefore, if you went to South London in the afternoon, you had to return to North London by nine o'clock in the evening, or you would have to pay a boatman to ferry you across the river.

At the south end of the bridge, there was a strange sight. On the top of long poles, there were round shapes which looked like heads. They had hair, and teeth, and ears, and noses. In fact, they were heads. If you were a traitor to Queen Elizabeth, your head would be chopped off and stuck on a pole, then left on London Bridge until you had completely rotted away.

Love On the Bridge
How Edward Osbourne found his wife.
An Amazing True Story.

One of London's Lord Mayors lived on London Bridge. His name was William Hewitt. He and his wife had three sons and a daughter. She was a little baby, who had a nursemaid specially to look after her. Every day, the nursemaid would hold the girl out of the window, and show her everything that was happening on the river. 'Look at those boats! Look at the swans! Look at that man swimming!' One day, the nurse's hands were slippery, and she dropped the baby. The baby fell straight down into the water, and landed with a

SPLASH!

Edward Osbourne was the son of a country gentleman. He worked as an apprentice to William Hewitt. He jumped off the bridge, plunged into the water, and rescued the little girl...

Sixteen years later, the girl had grown up into a beautiful woman. Men came from all over London to woo her, and ask her father for her hand in marriage. Even the Earl of Shrewsbury, a wealthy and important man, wanted to marry her.

But she didn't marry any of them. Instead, she married Edward Osbourne, the man who had rescued her from drowning.

Squalid Southwark

On the other side of the bridge, after you passed the heads and went through the gate, you entered South London. The area was called Southwark. In fact, it still is called Southwark.

Today, when you go to Southwark, the main street is called

40

Borough High Street. In Shakespeare's time, Borough High Street was the route to the South Coast. From there, you would catch a coach to Brighton, Bognor or any of the towns in Kent and Sussex. London Bridge was locked at 9 o'clock every night, so if you wanted to catch an early coach, or you arrived late at night, you had to stay in Southwark. For all the travellers, there were a lot of cheap hotels and even more cheap pubs.

A famous writer, Thomas Dekker, described Borough High Street as 'a continued ale house with not a shop to be seen between'.

The most famous pubs were called the Bear, the Queen's Head, the George, the White Hart and the Tabard. None of them are still standing, although there's a pub called The George in Borough High Street.

If you kept walking down the High Street, you came to a big building with no windows. That was a prison. Southwark had five prisons, but this was the biggest and the best. It was called Marshalsea Prison. After the Tower of London, it was the most important prison in London.

In 1605, three playwrights were locked up there: Ben Jonson, George Chapman and John Marston. Together, they had written a play called *Eastward Hoe*, which was full of jokes about the stupidity of Scottish people. This was a pretty stupid thing to do because at the time King James I was the king. There are two things that everybody should know about King James I: firstly, he was Scottish; secondly, he wasn't the sort of king who liked laughing at himself. So he had the three playwrights arrested and threw them into prison.

Apart from pubs and the prison, all kinds of foul-smelling businesses were dumped in Southwark. If you wanted to build a factory to make soap or boil animal skins, then you went to Southwark. There, the smells were whisked away by the river's breezes, so they were less likely to get up the noses of the posh people in North London.

Most of Southwark was owned by the Church. This meant that many bishops had their official residences here, including the Bishops of Winchester and Rochester. Strangely this meant that the whole area was given over to illegal activities. If you wanted to have fun, and didn't care whether you broke a few laws, then you went to Southwark. So, this was the perfect place to build a theatre.

Because so much land in Southwark was owned by the Church, normal laws didn't apply. You could do what you liked. In a strange way, the presence of the Church encouraged people to behave badly. If you were a Londoner, and you wanted to have fun, you would go to Southwark.

THE CARDENIO CHRONICLE
SPORTS PAGES
WHAT'S ON IN LONDON THIS WEEK

By our special sports
correspondent, Inigo Boot

It's a good week for
sport in London. No
sports-lover will be bored.
Whatever you like to
watch - fighting dogs,
fighting men, fighting bears
- they're all here.

Bullfight
New bulls every day. Free
steak after the fight for
all ticket-holders. Tickets:
one penny to stand up,
two pennies if you want to sit down.

Dogfight
We have three new dogs for this week's fight: Lucky, Gnasher
and Pob. Only one will survive! Your excitement guaranteed!
Current odds: Lucky 4-1, Gnasher 3-2, Pop 2-1. Place your bets
now! Tickets: as for bullfight.

Bear-baiting
See the bear fight dogs! See the bear fight bulls! See the bear
fight other bears! Our famous bear, Bruno, has been fighting
for three years, and he has only lost twice! Tickets: as for
bullfight.

Archery

Hit the bullseye and win a prize! Bring your own bow. Prizes: one penny for the winner, a chicken for the runner-up. Tickets: Free.

Wrestling

A variety of English and foreign wrestlers will be fighting thoughout the week. Tonight: Fat French Francois takes on the English Giant. Tickets: two pennies.

Hanging

On Saturday only one man will be hanged. Gary Stup stole a pig. He will be hanged by the neck until he is dead. This promises to be a lot of fun. Tickets: free. Bring a picnic.

CHAPTER SIX

The Globe

Do you remember Cuthbert and Richard Burbage? When we last saw them, they were pushing a cart filled with wood across London Bridge. They crossed the river and went into Southwark. On a plot of land near the river, they unloaded the wood and started building. Lots of people helped them. Shakespeare probably helped too, unless he was too busy writing. They built a tall, round structure. A new theatre. They decided to call it the Globe.

No one knows why they chose that name. But it's a good name for a theatre. When you're inside a theatre, you could be anywhere. On the stage, the actors might be sailing through a vicious storm, fighting a battle in France, or standing on the ramparts of a castle in Denmark. You just have to use your imagination a little, and you could be anywhere on Earth.

Anywhere on the globe.

The Globe was owned by eight people. These are their names: Richard Burbage, Cuthbert Burbage, Nicholas Brend, John Heminges, Augustine Philips, Thomas Pope, William Kemp and William Shakespeare. Together, they worked in the Globe and took some of the profits from selling tickets.

TODAY ONLY:

THE MOST TEAR-JERKING TRAGEDY OF

HAMLET, PRINCE OF DENMARK

A new play by Mister William Shakespeare

An excellent new play by our famous writer, Mister William Shakespeare, often described as 'the toast of the London stage'. His latest play will not disappoint his fans.

Hamlet is a Prince in Denmark. Will he take revenge for his father's death? Will he travel to England? Will he be killed by pirates? Will he marry the beautiful Ophelia? You can only discover by coming to the Globe, and watching the play for yourself.

ADDED ATTRACTIONS:

This play contains fighting with swords, fighting with fists, death by drowning, death by poison, death by bleeding, a love scene, and several jokes.

TICKET PRICES AS FOLLOWS:

Entrance to the theatre: one penny.
(You will be permitted to stand down at the bottom, near the stage, in the pit.)

Entrance to the theatre AND the hire of a seat: two pennies.

Entrance to the theatre AND the hire of a seat AND a cushion: three pennies.

Entrance to the theatre AND the hire of a seat AND a cushion AND the best seats in the house: sixpence.
(You will be permitted to sit on the stage, right next to the actors.)

A Good Night Out?

The cheapest seats in the Globe cost one penny. Nowadays the cheapest seats for a theatre in the West End cost £16. That's 1,600 pennies. In other words, for the price of one night in today's West End, you could have seen 1,600 performances in the Globe. That's one performance every day for four and a half years.

Like the other theatres in London, the Globe had no roof. In bad weather, the performances would be cancelled. How did people know whether the play had been cancelled? You just had to look across the river, and see if the flag was flying. If the performance had been cancelled, the flag would be removed. If the flag was flapping in the breeze, then you would jump into a boat and cross the river.

When the play was just about to begin, a trumpeter would blow three blasts on his trumpet.

In modern theatres, the plays are performed at night. The audience sits in darkness, and the actors are illuminated by powerful lights. In Shakespeare's time, there was no electricity, so plays were rarely performed at night. Instead people would go to plays in the afternoons.

Do you remember Thomas Platter? He was the Swiss man who visited London, and wrote a book describing what he had seen. Well, he went to the theatre several times. This is what he wrote:

> '*On September 21st after lunch, about two o'clock, I and my party crossed the water, and there in the house with the thatched roof witnessed an excellent performance of the tragedy of the first Emperor Julius Caesar with a cast of some fifteen people; when the play was over, they danced very marvellously and gracefully together as is their wont, two dressed as men and two as women.*'

Julius Caesar is one of Shakespeare's plays. (For the rest of his plays, see the list at the end of the book.)

A Day in the Life of Thomas Crumble

Thomas Crumble was an actor at the Globe. He got his first job at the age of twelve. As a pretty young boy, he was perfect to play women. Unfortunately, his voice broke when he was fifteen, and he started growing a beard, so he had to play men rather than women. Here is a typical day in his life.

7 – Wake up. My head hurts. Must be all that beer I drank last night.

8 – Breakfast on hot water and a nice fresh sardine

8.30 – Wash my face in cold water. Soon, it will be July, when I have my annual bath. Is it really so long? Seems like much longer.

10 – Spend some time remembering my lines from the play.

12.30 – A quick snack of cheese and a glass of beer.

2 – The play starts. It is *Hamlet* by Will Shakespeare. I play Horatio and a few other small parts. Good audience. They don't talk too much during the action.

4 – The play finishes. When the audience has gone, I find a penny that someone has dropped then half a potato. Harry Retch tried to fight me for the potato, but I beat him.

5 – Rehearsal for tomorrow. We do a different play every day. Tomorrow, it will be *Two Noble Kinsmen*. I have twenty-eight lines, but I know them already.

7 – Dinner. A steak pie and a small glass of beer.

8 – Down to the tavern with some of the other actors. The Burbage brothers are there, and Will Kemp, who dances on the tables with a couple of the girls. Two small glasses of beer. Then two more. After that, I lost count.

10 – To bed. My head is spinning. Dream that Burbage has asked me to play Hamlet. When I wake up, I'm so disappointed that I have to drink a small glass of beer.

You know the way that modern theatres are like churches? Everyone sits in silence, don't they? Well, Shakespeare's theatres weren't like that. Because the plays were performed outside, the audience weren't quiet. They would have chatted during the plays. Lots of other noises would have disturbed the actors too. Birds flying overhead. Horses neighing. Carts clattering down the street. People selling things, and shouting out their advertisements for what they were selling.

'Luverly oranges! Who wants to buy my luverly oranges! Only a penny for five!'

'Fresh fish! Caught this morning! Who wants to buy some nice fresh fish?'

During the play, people would walk around, selling apples, beer, cakes and tobacco.

Sometimes, the play would be interrupted by someone shouting. 'Pickpocket! Pickpocket!' The actors would stop in mid-sentence. Everyone would chase the pickpocket. When he was caught, the play would start again, and the pickpocket would be chained to a post on the stage. He would sit there throughout the play. Everyone would laugh at

him. They would throw things at him, or tickle him. That would teach him never to steal again!

At other times, the play would be interrupted by people shouting at the actors. For instance, in *Othello*, there is a scene where Iago lies to Othello. It's a horrible scene, and, watching it, you can't help feeling very sorry for Othello because after that bit things go terribly wrong for him. At that point in the play, someone might have jumped up and shouted:

'Don't believe him! He's lying! Don't believe a word that he says!'

At other times, people would have let the actors know what they thought of the characters. When a villain or a Frenchman came onto the stage, the audience BOOED and HISSED. When an actor asked a question, the audience would shout the answer. If you go to a performance at the Globe today, you will discover that the same thing happens. The audience gets involved in the play. It's a lot of fun. If you ever thought that plays were boring, just take a trip to the Globe. You'll quickly discover how wrong you were.

There were only two other things that would stop the play. The first was fire. If there was a fire in the theatre, everyone would run outside; the Globe was made of wood, so it burnt fast. In fact, in 1613, a fire started during a performance at the Globe. Here is a passage from a letter written at that time, which describes exactly what happened:

No longer since than yesterday, when Burbage's company were acting at the Globe the play of Henry VIII, and there shooting off certain chambers in way of triumph, the fire catched and fastened upon the thatch of the house, and there burned so furiously, as it consumed the whole house, all in less than two hours, the people having enough to do to save themselves.

Thomas Larkin, letter to Sir Thomas Puckering, 30 June 1613

In other words, there was a performance of a play called
Henry VII at the Globe. (This was a play that Shakespeare wrote
in partnership with another writer, a man called John Fletcher.)
When a cannon was fired during the performance, some sparks
landed on the theatre's roof, and lit the thatch. Within two
hours, the whole place had burnt down. People couldn't save
the theatre, because they were so worried about saving
themselves. In fact, only one person was hurt: his trousers
caught fire, and he got a burnt bum. Luckily, someone threw a
pint of beer over him, and put out the fire. So he got a wet
burnt bum. Great! The Globe itself wasn't so lucky, and it
burned to the ground. A year later, it was rebuilt.

The second thing that would shut the theatres was the plague.

The theatres would shut if more than thirty people died from the plague in one week. Often, many more people died. In 1593, 10,000 people died from the plague. In 1603, over 25,000 died. From 1603 to 1604, the Globe closed for eleven months. The actors didn't go on holiday. Instead, they toured around the rest of England, taking Shakespeare's plays to people who didn't live in London.

The Globe wasn't the only place where Shakespeare and his company performed their plays. Sometimes, Elizabeth wanted to watch a play. She was the Queen of England, so she didn't go to the theatre. The theatre went to her. All the actors packed their costumes, and went to one of her palaces.

WHAT'S PLAYING IN LONDON?

A guide to the best new plays on the London stage
By our drama critic, Cecil Fopmeister

Just like last year, no one in London wants to watch a play written by anyone except our favourite writer, Mister William Shakespeare. This week, you can catch no less than SIX of his plays around town. Here's a quick plot summary of each of them:

A Midsummer Night's Dream

In the middle of the summer, the forest is full of people: lovers from the city, some workmen rehearsing a play, and the King and Queen of the fairies. There's a great scene where a man is turned into a donkey. This is the funniest play that I have ever seen. Beg, buy or steal a ticket - you have to see this play!

Romeo and Juliet

Romeo loves Juliet. Juliet loves Romeo. There's just one problem: their families hate each other. There's a good scene on a balcony, and some great sword fights. It ends unhappily.

Henry IV Part One

The King has lost his son, Prince Hal. We know where he is: he's wandering round London, getting drunk with his fat friend Falstaff. But when the war starts, Prince Hal has to make a choice: is he going to continue having a good time or start taking responsibility for himself?

Henry IV Part Two

A sequel to Henry IV Part One. Prince Hal is older, but not much wiser. The war continues. Falstaff keeps drinking. At the end, Prince Hal makes his choice between fun and responsibility. What do you think he chooses? To find out, you'll have to see the play.

King Lear

An old King has three daughters. He promises to give his kingdom to the one who loves him most. His plan goes horribly wrong, and leads to death, war and more death. I didn't really understand what it was all about, but there are some quite good jokes.

Macbeth

Three witches making soup meet a Scottish nobleman, and make him a promise. Should he trust them? And what about his wife? Is she mad? Why does she keep sleepwalking? This gory play has several deaths, a ghost and a lot of violence. Not suitable for under-fives.

CHAPTER SEVEN

Your Palace or Mine?

Nowadays, Westminster is part of London. In fact, many people think that it is the very centre of London. However, when Shakespeare lived in London, Westminster was a separate little town outside the city.

In the heart of Westminster, there were lots of buildings belonging to the royal family. Of them all, Henry VIII – the king who had six wives – preferred Whitehall Palace, and he made it into the biggest palace in Europe. After his death, his children continued adding more and more buildings, creating a series of large, luxurious homes for themselves.

When it was his daughter Elizabeth's turn to be Queen, she added several banqueting halls. In the Great Hall, Queen Elizabeth watched a lot of plays which had been written by Shakespeare, who acted in them too. When James I came to the throne, he decreed that an annual play should be performed for his pleasure. He chose All Saints' Day – 1 November – as the day, and Whitehall as the place.

During these performances, men like Shakespeare would have been allowed inside the royal palaces. It was their only chance. Normally, they wouldn't even have got through the door.

Postcards from the Palaces

In 1998, historians in Gloucester searched an old cupboard in the cathedral and discovered a dusty box containing several letters and postcards. They were five hundred years old. They had been written by Thomas Crumble, an actor in London, to his mother.

Thomas Crumble acted in many of Shakespeare's plays. In his postcards, he describes visiting many palaces in and around London. There, the actors performed Shakespeare's plays to Queen Elizabeth, King James, and many other important people.

December 3rd

Dear Mum,
The tour is going very well. Today, we're playing
Titus Andronicus another play by Mister
Shakespeare. It's called . I have twelve lines.
We have done the play in Whitehall Palace. It's
very big. I had scrambled eggs for supper, and an
apple.
Thanks for the socks.
Love from your son,

Thomas X

December 19th

Dear Mum,

We've been performing in Greenwich Palace. It's very beautiful, and I've learnt all kinds of interesting things about the place. It stands in the middle of a wide open park. Noblemen hunt here, riding beautiful horses, or using hawks to hunt down small prey such as rabbits.

This is where our great Queen Elizabeth was born. She certainly seems to love it here. Do you realize that she spends more time in this palace than any of her others? (And she's got a lot of palaces!)

The other day, Sir Walter Raleigh came to Greenwich to report to the Queen. As he hurried towards her, he saw that she was walking through some wet ground. He removed his cloak, and laid it on the mud for her to walk across. I saw this with my own eyes!

Anyway, I'd better go now. We have to rehearse for tomorrow. Mister Shakespeare complimented me yesterday, and promised to write some lines specially for me.

Thanks for the socks. Now, I have three pairs. That should last me the whole year!

Love from

Thomas

January 4th

Dear Mum,

We performed in Hampton Court Palace last night. It's very beautiful. The river flows past the end of the gardens. The air is quiet. This palace was King Henry VIII's favourite; it was originally built by Cardinal Wolsey. Did you know that?

If possible, could you send something other than socks? I only have two feet, you know.

Love from

Thomas

January 18th

Dear Mum,

The tour is going very well. I made Mister Shakespeare very happy by giving him some socks! He only had one pair to last him the whole year, so he was very pleased to get some more. (Hope you don't mind!)

We're in Richmond. There's a beautiful palace here. Did you know that when horrible Bloody Mary was Queen of England, she imprisoned her sister in Richmond Palace? I suppose that's one of the useful things about being Queen: if your brother or sister gets irritating, you can just lock them up.

A strange and wonderful man lives nearby in Mortlake. His name is Dr John Dee, and he is a famous magician. He has a long white beard. Last night, he came to see the show. Afterwards, he removed a white rabbit from Mister Shakespeare's hat. Mister Shakespeare is going to keep the rabbit as a pet. He has named it Miranda.

Tomorrow, we'll get in the boat and return to Southwark. I'm looking forward to seeing the Globe again.

Thank you for the hat. I am wearing it now. It's very warm!

Love from your loving son,

Thomas

How to Avoid the Congestion Charge in 1599

Queen Elizabeth travelled around London by boat, because the river was faster than any of the roads. By boat, Elizabeth could visit all the places that were most important to her: Hampton Court Palace, Whitehall, Somerset House, the Tower of London and Greenwich Palace. From Greenwich to Hampton Court is about eighteen miles by car. Nowadays, you can still do the same journey in a boat. (*For details, see p.95*)

Queen Elizabeth would have travelled in the Royal Barge. There is a famous map of Elizabethan London which has a little picture of the Royal Barge. It is a slim boat without a sail or oars. It is attached by a rope to another boat, which is pulling it along the river. Twelve oarsman are working very hard, pulling both boats. (If you go to the Museum of London, you can see this beautiful map, and look for the little drawing of the Royal Barge.)

Here are some lines from one of Shakespeare's plays called *Anthony and Cleopatra*. They describe Cleopatra travelling down the river in a boat, but they could easily be a description of Elizabeth in her boat on the Thames.

The barge she sat in, like a burnish'd throne,

Burn'd on the water: the poop was beaten gold;

Purple the sails, and so perfumed that

The winds were love-sick with them; the oars were silver,

Which to the tune of flutes kept stroke, and made

The water which they beat to follow faster,

As amorous of their strokes.

CHAPTER EIGHT

Lock Him in the Tower!

The Tower is one of the few buildings in London that hasn't changed much since Shakespeare's time. Well, some things have changed. In Shakespeare's time, the Tower had a zoo. In 1598, this contained two lions, a wolf, an eagle, a porcupine, a tiger and a lynx. Also, dead criminals and pirates would be executed in the Tower, and left to rot, hanging by chains from the walls. The smell must have been terrible!

Shakespeare knew the Tower well. In his plays, the building is mentioned more often than any other building. Shakespeare repeated the myth that the Tower had been built by Julius Caesar. These are the words of the Queen in Richard II:

> This is the way the king will come; this is the way
> To Julius Caesar's ill-erected tower,
> To whose flint bosom, my condemned lord,
> Is doomed a prisoner by proud Bolingbroke.

Julius Caesar didn't really build the Tower of London. In fact, William the Conqueror began building it after his invasion in 1066.

The Tower was originally built as a fortress. It has been used as a jail, a treasury, a zoo, the Royal Mint, the Armouries, the Royal Observatory, and a home for various kings and queens of England. Now, it is a museum. The Crown Jewels have been kept there since 1303, you can still see them there today.

Over the centuries, many people have been imprisoned in the Tower. Queen Elizabeth was imprisoned there during the reign of her sister, Queen Mary. Later, when Elizabeth became Queen, she used the Tower as a prison and a place of execution. As you might imagine, she didn't fancy living in the Tower, because she'd already spent some time there as a prisoner. Instead, she sent her enemies there. When the Earl of Essex led a rebellion against her, he was imprisoned and executed there.

Walter Raleigh

One of the Tower's most famous prisoners was Walter Raleigh. He was imprisoned in 1592 by Queen Elizabeth for seducing and marrying one of her maids of honour, Lizzie Throckmorton. Eventually, Elizabeth forgave Raleigh, and released him. He took a ship, and sailed across the Atlantic. When he got to the other side, he explored the Americas. In Virginia, he founded the first European colony. (Queen Elizabeth's nickname was 'The Virgin Queen' – which is why he named the colony Virginia.) Later, he won a great victory against the Spanish Fleet.

After the death of Elizabeth, James became king. He imprisoned Raleigh for a second time, throwing him back in the Tower. Raleigh lived there for thirteen years, from 1603 to 1616. During that time, he wrote his book, *The History of the World*. It was a strange kind of imprisonment. He was allowed to have visitors, and his wife and son lived with him. He could take walks on the Tower's grass. However, he could never leave the walls.

In 1604, King James I wrote a book called A *Counterblast to Tobacco*. He described smoking like this:

'A *custom loathsome to the eye, hateful to the nose, harmful to the brain, dangerous to the lungs, and in the black, stinking fume thereof, nearest resembling the horrible Stygian smoke of the pit that is bottomless. Herein it is not only a great vanity, but a great contempt of God's good gifts, that the sweetness of man's breath, being a good gift of God, should be wilfully corrupted by this stinking smoke.'*

Maybe that's why King James didn't like Raleigh – because Raleigh had brought tobacco from South America to England.

In 1618, James changed his mind, and allowed Raleigh to leave the Tower. Then, he changed his mind again. This time, he wanted it to be final. He brought Raleigh back to the Tower and chopped off his head.

If you go to the Tower today, perhaps you will see the ghost of a man. If he's smoking a pipe, and carrying his head under his arm, then you'll know who he is.

Constable Catchpole

HELP! HELP! Call the police! I'm being murdered!

Sorry, I can't call the police.

Why not?

Because they haven't been invented yet.

At night, the streets of London were patrolled by a watchman, armed with a halberd. (A halberd is like an axe with a long handle. The head of the axe has a hook on its back. In other words, it's a vicious weapon.) The watchman would enforce the laws. These are some of the laws that he enforced, and the punishments that he would give.

After dark, you may not whistle.
(Punishment: a fine of one penny)

After dark, you may not shout.
(Punishment: a fine of two pennies.)

After dark, you may not
blow a horn.
(Punishment: a fine of
sixpence or a week in
prison.)

After dark, you may not
cause any disturbance that
will wake people up.
(Punishment: one day in
prison for every person that you
wake up.)

CHAPTER NINE

St Paul's Cathedral

During Shakespeare's time, there were at least one hundred churches in London. No one would dispute which was the biggest and greatest of them: it was St Paul's Cathedral.

St Paul's has been built many times. It was founded by King Ethelbert in 640, then burnt down in 1287. It was built again, little by little, and, by Shakespeare's time, it was the longest church in Europe.

When the cathedral was built, it had a tall spire, with a copper weather-cock on the top to show which way the wind was blowing. For a penny, you could pay to climb the spire, and see the whole of London. However, the spire was hit by a flash of lightning and burnt down. By the time that Shakespeare came to London, it still had not been rebuilt. So the cathedral had no spire.

What do you do in a church? Pray? Sing hymns? Think about God? Well, that stuff did happen in St Paul's, but lots of other things happened there too.

In the churchyard, people had little shops. Some of the shops sold books. Books were very expensive, so only rich people could afford them. Poorer people would buy pamphlets for a penny. Or you could buy sheets of riddles, which you could use to puzzle and entertain your friends. You could buy books of songs and poems. You could buy books describing amazing voyages or new scientific discoveries.

In fact, from the booksellers around St Paul's, you could buy almost every book that had ever been published. These booksellers were the first people to publish anything by Shakespeare. The first editions of his poems, *Venus and Adonis* and *Rape of Lucrece*, were published by a bookseller called John Harrison. This was also the place to buy Shakespeare's plays. Sometimes, people bought a copy of the play and took it to the theatre. Then, if they couldn't understand what the actors were saying, they could just follow the story in the book.

Other shops sold lottery tickets, just like the National Lottery. However, the prizes were smaller. In fact, the first lottery in Britain was held in St Paul's churchyard in 1569. The biggest prize was £5000, and the tickets were ten shillings (in other words, 50p). How many tickets do you think were sold?

70

And how many tickets do you think are sold each week in the modern National Lottery? (The answers are 400,000 and about 10 million.) Just like today, a lot of the money went towards good causes. In 1569 the money was used for repairing harbours throughout England.

Some Riddles From Books Sold in the Yard of St Paul's

1. QUESTION: What is the cleanest leaf of all the leaves?
   ANSWER: It is the holly leaf, for no one will wipe his bum with a holly leaf.

2. QUESTION: What beast is it that has her tail between her eyes?
   ANSWER: It is a cat, when she licks her bum.

3. QUESTION: How many calves' tails does it take to reach from the earth to the sky?
   ANSWER: No more than one, if it is long enough.

Occasionally, criminals were executed in the churchyard of St Paul's. In 1606, some men tried to blow up the Houses of Parliament. Among them, there was a Yorkshireman called Guy Fawkes. We now remember him on Bonfire Night. Several of his friends were hanged in front of St Paul's Cathedral.

Inside the church, you might have found a few people praying or singing hymns, but you would have found other people eating, drinking and talking. And not just people. Horses and cows also wandered through the church – until a law was passed, forbidding any animals from entering the nave. But that didn't stop people misbehaving in the church. Some of them argued. Others fought duels.

If you had something to sell, you could wander up and down the church, trying to find a customer. It didn't matter what you were selling. Lawyers sold their knowledge of the law. Cooks sold food. Tailors sold cloth and lace. Some people even sold themselves. For instance, if you were a servant without a job, you might find a new master inside the cathedral.

In 1666, fifty years after Shakespeare's death, St Paul's burnt down in the Great Fire of London. After the fire, Sir Christopher Wren designed a new building – also called St Paul's Cathedral – which is still standing in London.

Penny Dictionary

all the words you could need for a penny
Buy the Penny Dictionary *at Terry's Books, Number 3, St Paul's*
Churchyard. Ask for Terry.

FAP – drunk
Suggested usage: 'Stop drinking, you fat fap!'

COZEN – to cheat
Suggested usage: 'I lost six pounds at cards – but I was cozened.'

A COZENER – someone who cheats
Suggested usage: 'That dirty cozener got six pounds off me in a game of snap.'

A LIFTER – a thief
Suggested usage: 'Stop! Lifter! He's lifted my best apples!'

A NATURAL – an idiot
Suggested usage: 'You natural! No wonder you've made such a mess! You have to break the eggs before you scramble them!'

A POPINJAY – a parrot or a talkative person
Suggested usage: 'Have you seen my popinjay? He flew out of the window this morning, and he hasn't been seen since.'

A WAT – a hare
Suggested usage: 'What? A wat? Running through the market? Catch that wat and we'll make a wat pot for dinner!'

(Editor's note. You can use these words at your own risk. DO NOT use them to anyone who is more than four hundred years old. They will know what the words mean, and you will insult them horribly.)

CHAPTER TEN

Shakespeare's Friends

This chapter concentrates on three men who were friends with Shakespeare. One of them died young, one of them might have killed Shakespeare, and one of them never even existed.

Christopher Marlowe

Christopher Marlowe was a great playwright. His most famous plays are called *The Jew of Malta*, *Doctor Faustus* and *Tamburlaine*. They are often performed today. He was a brilliant playwright, but he died very young, so he only had time to write a few plays.

One day in the spring of 1593, Christopher Marlowe travelled to East London. He went to Deptford. There, he found a nice pub and ordered some beer.

Four men spent the day drinking in that pub. They were two servants, a secret agent of the Government and Christopher Marlowe. They ate a meal together, then argued about the bill, and started fighting. Someone drew a dagger. A minute later, Marlowe lay on the floor, dead. No one knows why he was killed. There are lots of different theories. Marlowe was a brilliant young playwright, but he might have been a spy too. He was definitely an atheist. (In other words, he did not believe in God.) Some people think that he was murdered on the orders of Queen Elizabeth.

If Christopher Marlowe hadn't been killed, he might have become even more famous than Shakespeare. Instead, he had a strong influence on Shakespeare's own plays.

Ben Jonson

Ben Jonson was another famous playwright. He lived much longer than Christopher Marlowe so he had a chance to write all kinds of interesting things. He worked as a bricklayer, a soldier and an actor, then started writing plays.

He killed a man in a duel. He was put in prison because of what he wrote in his plays. Altogether, he had a very exciting life.

There's a legend that Ben Jonson was connected to Shakespeare's death.

The legend goes like this. Apparently, Ben Jonson travelled to Stratford to visit Shakespeare. That night, they went to the pub. They drank a lot. They stayed up all night. It was just like old times. Then, they staggered back to Shakespeare's house and fell asleep.

In the morning, Jonson woke up with a terrible hangover. Shakespeare didn't wake up at all. The drink had killed him. No one knows if this legend is true or not.

Sir John Falstaff

Sir John Falstaff was a huge fat man. He loved eating and drinking. He hated working. If he needed some money, he stole it from his enemies or borrowed it from his friends. His best friend was Prince Henry – also known as young Prince Hal – who would one day be the King of England.

Sir John Falstaff never really existed. He is a character who appears in several of Shakespeare's plays. He is such a great character that other writers and artists have borrowed him, and used him in their plays too. An opera is named after him. Pictures have been painted of him. He has appeared in films and books. While Shakespeare's real friends have been dead for hundreds of years, his imaginary friend has continued living until today, and will stay alive long into the future.

Sir John Falstaff appears in several plays, but his greatest moments are in a wonderful play called Henry IV, which is divided into two parts. If you haven't seen these two plays, you should do so as soon as possible. You won't be disappointed.

A Night in the Tavern

Hal and Falstaff spent most of their time in the pub. They often went to a pub called the Boar's Head Tavern. In Henry IV Part One, this is where Falstaff, Prince Hal and the other drinkers meet. They plot a robbery, get drunk, sing, dance, and generally have a wonderful time.

This is the beginning of a scene in *Richard* II, where Prince Hal's father, Henry Bolingbroke, is fretting over what has happened to his son, worrying that he is spending too much time in London pubs. Which is exactly what he was doing.

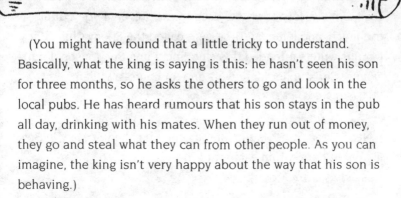

Enter **HENRY BOLINGBROKE, HENRY PERCY**, and other Lords

HENRY BOLINGBROKE:

Can no man tell me of my unthrifty son?
'Tis full three months since I did see him last;
If any plague hang over us, 'tis he.
I would to God, my lords, he might be found:
Inquire at London, 'mongst the taverns there,
For there, they say, he daily doth frequent,
With unrestrained loose companions,
Even such, they say, as stand in narrow lanes,
And beat our watch, and rob our passengers;
Which he, young wanton and effeminate boy,
Takes on the point of honour to support
So dissolute a crew.

(You might have found that a little tricky to understand. Basically, what the king is saying is this: he hasn't seen his son for three months, so he asks the others to go and look in the local pubs. He has heard rumours that his son stays in the pub all day, drinking with his mates. When they run out of money, they go and steal what they can from other people. As you can imagine, the king isn't very happy about the way that his son is behaving.)

79

The Boar's Head Tavern was in Eastcheap, near Pudding Lane. This is where, in 1666, the Great Fire of London was started by a careless baker. The pub was destroyed in the fire of London, 1666, then rebuilt in stone rather than wood, and finally demolished in 1831 to clear the path for the new London Bridge.

In the pub, Falstaff and his friends would not only drink, but also play games. They might play cards. Or they would roll dice. Or they would sing. Of course, there weren't any tapes or CDs in those days. If you wanted to hear some music, you had to make it yourself. So, everyone was pretty good at singing.

Not far from Pudding Lane, you would have found Bread Street. There was another famous pub in Bread Street: the Mermaid Tavern. It also burnt down in the Great Fire of 1666. In the Mermaid, lots of writers used to meet every Friday, drink too much, and fall over. They were called the Friday Club. Many famous writers attended this club, including Ben Jonson, John Donne, Christopher Marlowe – and, of course, William Shakespeare.

Near Bread Street is the famous church called St Mary le Bow. If you are born within earshot of these bells, then you are classed as a true Cockney.

Bartholomew Fair

When Falstaff was bored with the pub, he would have gone looking for some more fun. Maybe he would have gone to the theatre in Southwark. More likely, he walked north to Smithfield, where the whole of London came for duels, fights and other sports.

Smithfield was a big open field. It was used for tournaments, jousting and sporting events like wrestling, duels and fighting. If anyone found a witch, she would be burned or boiled alive in Smithfield. While the witch was being burnt or boiled, a priest would stand nearby, waiting for her to confess her sins.

Once a year, on 24 August, a huge fair was held in Smithfield. It was called Bartholomew Fair. The first one was held in 1123. When the fair started, it was intended for merchants to sell their cloth. However, over the centuries, the fair changed, and became more frivolous. It was like a modern fun fair. There was juggling, games and all kinds of entertainments. Ben Jonson wrote a play about the fair. You won't be surprised to learn that the play is called *Bartholomew Fair*.

The fairs continued until 1855, when the Victorians shut it down. Nowadays, the site of Bartholomew Fair is being converted into a big office block.

The Puritans

The Puritans were a group of people who hated fun. They didn't like having fun, and they didn't like the idea of other people having fun. Whenever they could, they tried to stop fun. During Shakespeare's lifetime, and afterwards, there was a struggle between two groups of people. On one side, there were the Puritans. On the other side, there were people who liked having fun.

In 1642, the Purtains won this battle. They stopped all fun in London. They closed down all the theatres. They banned dancing. They stopped bear-baiting and bullfights.
If the Puritans had stopped bullfights and bear-baiting because they thought people shouldn't be cruel to animals, that would have been great. But they didn't. They stopped bullfights and bear-baiting because people enjoyed them.

As you might imagine, people didn't like not being allowed to have fun. After a few years, they kicked out the Puritans, and brought back fun. The theatres opened. Everyone started dancing. It was all such fun!

And what happened to the Puritans? Well, they carried on trying to stop anyone having fun. In fact, they still exist. If you see them, just put a big smile on your face, and start dancing. There's nothing that Puritans hate more than smiling and dancing.

THE PURITAN MANIFESTO

Stop fun! No more fun! Ban fun! Stop all fun! That's it.

The Rules of Football

There was another good way to have fun if you were Elizabethan: playing a game of football. Often, two villages would play against each other. They would play on a large field. The ball would be a pig's bladder, filled with air. These were the rules:

RULE ONE - If you get the ball from one end of the field to the other, you win.

RULE TWO - There isn't a second rule.

RULE THREE - There isn't a third rule either, or a fourth. There is just one rule. If you get the ball from one end of the field to the other, you win. You can do whatever you want to get the ball from one end of the field to the other. You can pick up the ball, or kick it. You can hit other people. You can use your arms, your feet, your head. Everything is permitted.

It would take another three hundred years before people decided that football should have more than one rule.

THE DAILY DOGSBODY
SPORTS PAGES

FOOTBALL REPORT

By our special sports correspondent Inigo Boot

Last Saturday, there was a football match between men from Rotherhithe and a group of actors from Southwark. The game started with a kick-off. Several men kicked several other men. There were two broken legs within the first twenty seconds of the game. The ball went to Tom Brown, who ran three hundred yards before getting punched by one of the actors. He fell over. The ball went into the air. William Shakespeare caught the ball for the actors, then got beaten to the ground by twelve strong men.

Much fighting ensued. In the end, the men from Rotherhithe won the game.

End result: Rotherhithe 1, Actors 0.
Injuries: 0 deaths, 3 broken legs, 12 broken arms and shoulders, 27 bruised heads, 39 cuts and sores.
All in all, a very entertaining game.

CHAPTER ELEVEN

Eating and Drinking

The streets of London weren't just filled with people. They were filled with animals too. Wherever you went, you would have seen animals. What kind of animals? Well, firstly, there were the animals that people used as transport: horses, mules and donkeys. Secondly, there were cats and dogs, which were kept as pets. Thirdly, there were all the animals that were kept for eating: chickens, sheep, cows, pigs and all the other animals that people eat nowadays.

But you wouldn't have bought a piece of chicken in the supermarket. No, if you wanted your own meat, then you kept your own chicken. So the streets of London would have been packed with chickens, sheep, and all the other animals that you now only see on a farm.

If you wanted a bit of a change, then you would walk outside the walls of London to the fields and woods. There, you would find rabbits and deer. Rabbit stew, anyone? Or a nice slice of venison? If you were a good shot with a bow and arrow, you could shoot a rabbit for yourself every day.

Some Pottage, Sir?

What did Elizabethan Londoners eat? Well we know they loved
sweet things, and many of them had terrible teeth. We know
that they ate lots of cheese, milk, eggs and butter.

If you were rich, you would have eaten lots of meat and fish.
However, most people couldn't afford to eat meat more than
once or twice a week. Their diet was very simple: bread and
pottage. Bread and pottage for breakfast. Bread and pottage for
lunch. And for supper, they would have bread and pottage.
Pottage was like porridge with added vegetables.

Would You Like a Fork With Your Dinner?

By the time of Shakespeare, forks
had only just been introduced
to England. Most people ate
with a spoon or their
hands. Eating with a fork
was an Italian fashion and
didn't really become
common in England for
another two hundred years.
To an English man or woman,
there was nothing strange about
eating with your fingers.

However, everyone used spoons and knives. The Elizabethans
loved spoons. If you go to a museum with any Elizabethan
tableware, you will see all kinds of spoons. Rich people used
silver spoons. Poor people used pewter spoons. And the
poorest people used wooden spoons.

Usually, you would just eat with a knife and your fingers. You would cut up your food with the knife, and put it into your mouth with your fingers. Only a savage would put a knife in his mouth! When the meal was finished, you would wash your knife so it didn't go rusty.

Some Elizabethan recipes

French Toast

Requires eggs, salt, bread, butter, sugar.
Separate the yolks from the whites. Sprinkle the yolks with salt. Cut the bread into slices. Heat butter in a pan. Dip the bread in the yolks, then fry in the pan. When done, sprinkle sugar on top, and eat.

Gingerbread

Requires ginger, cloves, cinnamon, liquorice, bread crumbs, anise seeds.
Take a pint of honey. Add a dash of water. Add the bread crumbs and stir well. Add the powdered ginger, ground cloves, cinnamon, liquorice and anise seeds. Knead it. Put it in a mould. Eat it.

Table Manners

The Elizabethans were extremely strict about table manners. Apart from anything else, they spent a lot of money on their clothes, so they took great care not to get food on themselves. It was very important to be tidy. There would be a tablecloth to cover the table, and a napkin to cover your clothes. People usually shared crockery with other diners, so it was very rude to leave greasy fingerprints or lip marks on the cups or dishes. In some ways, the Elizabethans had very different manners to us. For instance, they didn't mind spitting. It was quite normal to spit on the floor. Also, no one thought it was rude to wipe your nose on your clothes.

Again, things would be different for the rich and the poor. If you were rich, you had lots of different dishes, served by servants. If you were poor, you just had one big bowl (usually filled with pottage), and everyone crowded round to eat from it. In a rich household, the servants wouldn't eat until everyone else had eaten whatever they wanted; then, the servants would get the leftovers.

CHAPTER TWELVE

Home to Stratford

Beyond the walls of London, there were fields and trees. If you got bored of the city, and wanted to sniff the fresh air of the countryside, you only needed to walk for a few minutes. Imagine the busy streets around Shaftesbury Avenue or King's Cross. During Shakespeare's time, these would have been farms. Rather than concrete and tarmac, the land would have been covered with grass and trees.

Shakespeare was born in a small country town, and knew the sights and smells of the countryside. In London, if he missed the countryside, he would only have to walk for ten or fifteen minutes to find himself among fields and trees. If he walked for a little longer, and climbed the hills of Highgate or Hampstead, he would have found himself in deep forests.

Some time after 1610, Shakespeare decided that he'd had enough of the big city. He'd had enough of the smells, the noise, the hustle and the bustle. He wanted to leave London. He returned to Stratford-upon-Avon. This time, he was a wealthy man, so he didn't need to walk.

Most likely, he took a coach. In the next few years, he did a little work on a couple of plays, but nothing serious. Like most people who retire from a busy life, he probably just relaxed. Maybe he took up gardening, bird-watching or chess.
Do you remember the legend about Ben Jonson? The legend says that Ben Jonson came to visit Shakespeare in 1616. That night, Shakespeare and Jonson went out drinking. They talked about old times, and stayed up all night, drinking more and more. The next morning, Jonson woke up with a terrible headache. Shakespeare didn't wake up at all.

But that's just a legend. No one really knows what happened. For whatever reason, on 23 April 1616, William Shakespeare died. A few days later, he was buried in his local church in Stratford.

Life after death

A few more things happened in London which are important for understanding Shakespeare's life.

After his death, two of his friends and fellow-actors, John Heminge and Henry Condell, published his plays. If they hadn't done that, we wouldn't know much about Shakespeare. So, everyone should be very grateful to Heminge and Condell. They sold the collected edition of Shakespeare's plays in the churchyard of St Paul's Cathedral. The book is called the First Folio. You can now see one of the few remaining copies if you visit the British Library.

A few years later, in 1633, someone suggested that Shakespeare's body should be dug up. He was such a great writer, they said, he should be buried in Westminster Abbey. Then, someone else noticed the words which had been carved on Shakespeare's tomb:

GOOD FREND FOR JESUS SAKE FORBEARE
TO DIGG THE DUST ENCLOASED HEARE:
BLESTE BE YE MAN YT SPARES THES STONES,
AND CURSED BE HE YT MOVES MY BONES..

In other words: 'Good friend, for Jesus's sake don't dig up the body that has been buried here. A blessing on whoever leaves this tombstone as it is, and a curse on anyone who moves my bones.'

So they decided to leave him where he was.

However, in 1740, a monument to Shakespeare was erected in Poet's Corner in Westminster Abbey. It lies alongside commemorations to other famous writers such as Geoffrey Chaucer, Charles Dickens, Henry James, John Milton, the Bronte sisters, Jane Austen, George Eliot, William Thackeray and Shakespeare's mate Ben Jonson.

If you go to Westminster Abbey, you can see all these memorials, and more. They are the greatest writers that Britain has ever seen, and Shakespeare was the greatest of them all.

A List of Shakespeare's Plays

Henry VI Part One

Henry VI Part Two

Henry VI Part Three

Richard III

Titus Andronicus

The Two Gentlemen of Verona

The Taming of the Shrew

The Comedy of Errors

Love's Labour's Lost

King John

Richard II

A Midsummer Night's Dream

The Merchant of Venice

The Merry Wives of Windsor

Much Ado About Nothing

As You Like It

Twelfth Night

Romeo and Juliet

Henry IV Part One

Henry IV Part Two

Henry V

Julius Caesar

Hamlet

Troilus and Cressida

All's Well That Ends Well

Measure for Measure

Othello

King Lear

Timon of Athens

Macbeth

Anthony and Cleopatra

Coriolanus

Pericles

Cymbeline

A Winter's Tale

The Tempest

(There are two more plays, Henry VIII and The Two Noble Kinsmen, which were probably written by Shakespeare. However, he wrote them with another writer, John Fletcher, so they haven't been included in this list.)

Places to Visit

Shakespeare would have recognized many of the names of streets, buildings and monuments in modern London. However, he wouldn't have recognized the city itself. Places have changed, but some of the names have remained the same. For instance, London Bridge has been rebuilt since Shakespeare's time. And, you won't be surprised to hear, traitor's heads are no longer displayed on poles on the south side of the bridge.

However, there are some places in London where you can see reminders of Shakespeare. A few buildings have become museums. Some statues of Shakespeare dot the streets. Most importantly, Shakespeare's theatre has been fully rebuilt, and, throughout the summer, you can watch plays in the Globe just as people would have done four hundred years ago.

Here is a short list of places in Shakespearean London that you might like to visit.

Shakespeare's Globe, New Globe Walk, Bankside, SE1 9DT.

www.shakespeares-globe.org. Tel 020 7902 1500.
A visit to the Globe is highly recommended. It is the best place in the world to see Shakespeare's plays – exactly where and how they would have been performed when he was alive. It's only open during the summer. Like the original Globe, the theatre doesn't have a roof, so it would get pretty cold in the winter. It sometimes gets wet in the summer, but that's part of the fun. The Globe Museum, attached to the Globe, also has lots of interesting exhibits about Shakespeare.

The Clink Prison Museum, 1 Clink Street, Southwark SE1 9DG.

www.clink.co.uk. Tel 020 7378 1558. This small museum very close to the Globe is well worth visiting. The Clink was a prison for hundreds of years; now, it's packed with gory exhibits like chains and handcuffs.

The Bear Gardens, Bear Gardens, SE1 9ED

The Bear Gardens – the site of the last bear-baiting ring on Bankside – are not usually open to the public. It's now used for classes connected to the Globe but if you manage to sneak inside you'll see a large, stuffed bear.

The Tower of London, Tower Hill, EC3N 4AB. www.hrp.org.uk.

Tel 020 7709 0765. Some parts of the Tower of London haven't changed much since 1066. If you visit now, you can see all kinds of interesting stuff, including the Crown Jewels. There's also a museum packed with interesting weapons and armour.

Southwark Cathedral, London Bridge, SE1 9DA. www.dswark.org.

Tel 020 7367 6700. This large, beautiful church is a few minutes' walk from The Globe or the Tower. There's a memorial to Shakespeare inside. You can also see the tomb of Shakespeare's brother, Edmund Shakespeare, who was buried here on 31 December 1607.

The George Inn, 77 Borough High Street, Southwark, SE1 1NH. If you're visiting Southwark Cathedral, you can walk down Borough High Street and have a look at the George. It's an old pub, which has beautiful galleries surrounding a little courtyard. You don't have to go inside the pub; you can sit outside, or just sneak through the gates to have a look at the galleries. When Shakespeare lived in London, pubs would have looked a bit like the George.

Ireland Yard, Blackfriars, EC4

On this site, Shakespeare bought a gatehouse for £140, which he left to his daughter in his will. She left it to her daughter, Elizabeth, who was the last descendant of Shakespeare. Elizabeth sold the gatehouse in 1667, and died a few years later. After that, nothing survived of Shakespeare except his plays. Nowadays, Ireland Yard is just an ordinary street in Blackfriars. There's nothing much to see. But if you're passing, you can stop, and look around, and remember that Shakespeare used to own a house on this exact spot.

The Museum of London, London Wall, EC2Y 5HN.

www.museumoflondon.org.uk. Tel 020 7600 3699. This is a great museum full of interesting exhibits about the history of London. The section of Shakespeare's London is only one small section of the museum, but the whole place is worth visiting.

Public Records Office, Kew, Richmond, Surrey TW9 4DU.

Shakespeare's Last Will and Testament is stored in the Public Records Office Museum in Kew. The museum also includes the Domesday Book and lots of other documents which are very important in British history.

Hampton Court Palace, East Moseley, Surrey, KT8 9AU. www.hrp.org.uk.

Tel 020 8781 9500. The royal palaces at Richmond and Whitehall no longer exist. Greenwich Palace was knocked down by Charles II, and rebuilt in a different style. If you visit Richmond, Whitehall or Greenwich today, you won't see any of the buildings that Shakespeare saw and Elizabeth loved. Nevertheless, they are all beautiful places which are worth seeing. However, Hampton Court hasn't changed so much. There are lots of newer buildings, but some of the Tudor ones have survived. If you go there, you will see many buildings constructed by King Henry VIII and Queen Elizabeth I. And you can get lost in the maze.

Westminster Pier, Victoria Embankment, SW1A 2JH

Just as Shakespeare and Elizabeth did, you can travel along the Thames by boat. It is still the best way to get around London, and you will see much more than you would in a tube or on a bus. You can get a boat at Westminster Pier, near the Houses of Parliament. From there, you can travel east to Greenwich or west to Richmond and Hampton Court.

You can see statues of Shakespeare – or just his head –
in the following places:

The Church of St Matthias, Poplar, Poplar High Street, E14 0AE.
The Church of St Mary Aldermanbury, Queen Victoria Street EC4
The Church of St Andrew-by-the-Wardrobe, Queen Victoria Street EC4
Hammersmith Public Library, Shepherds Bush Rd, W6 7AT
Westminster Abbey, Westminster, SW1P 3PA
The British Museum, Great Russell Street, Bloomsbury, WC1B 3DG
The Albert Memorial, Kensington Gardens, W2 2UH
Leicester Square, Westminster, WC2H